© 1989 Franklin Watts

First published in Great Britain in 1989 by
Franklin Watts
12a Golden Square
London W1

First published in the USA by
Franklin Watts Inc.
387 Park Avenue South
New York, NY. 10016

First published in Australia by
Franklin Watts Australia
14 Mars Road, Lane Cove
New South Wales 2066

UK ISBN: 0 86313 844 6
US ISBN: 0-531-10719-1
Library of Congress Catalog
Card No: 88-29668

Design: Edward Kinsey
Consultant: Michael Chinery

Printed in Italy by G. Canale & C S.p.A. - Turin

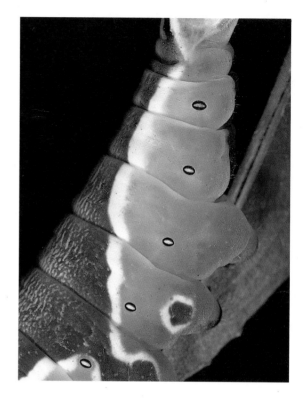

KEEPING MINIBEASTS

CATERPILLARS

TEXT AND PHOTOGRAPHS: BARRIE WATTS

CONTENTS

FRANKLIN WATTS
LONDON • NEW YORK • SYDNEY • TORONTO

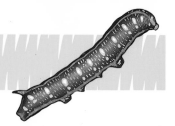

A caterpillar is the young stage of a butterfly or moth. Caterpillars are very colorful and some have smooth skins while others are very hairy.

Most caterpillars will eat only one type of plant. Their eggs must be laid on the correct food plant or else the young caterpillars will die when they hatch.

Habitats

Wherever you find butterflies or moths you will find caterpillars. There are almost 150,000 different species of caterpillars, and although most of them live on land, a few can also live under water.

Certain types of caterpillars feed only at night. During the day they hide in case they are eaten by birds. Caterpillars are protected to some extent by camouflage or tiny spines on their body.

Collecting

Caterpillars are easy to keep as pets. You can collect them from many types of plant. You can keep caterpillars in a jar or in a pet cage. The most important thing to remember is to keep them out of the sun.

Put some plant food in the container. It is important that caterpillars always have fresh food to eat. If not, they are unlikely to grow up and turn into the adult butterfly or moth.

Caterpillars are very fragile creatures. Some caterpillar hairs can cause skin rashes so it is best to move them using a small brush and a paper cup.

Caterpillars often cling to their food plant. Don't pull them off. Cut the leaf or twig on which they are sitting. They will soon crawl onto a fresh leaf when they are in the cage.

Housing

Caterpillars must be kept in good containers for them to grow properly, such as large glass or plastic jars or aquariums. The container must have a tight fitting lid with plenty of air holes to let any moisture escape.

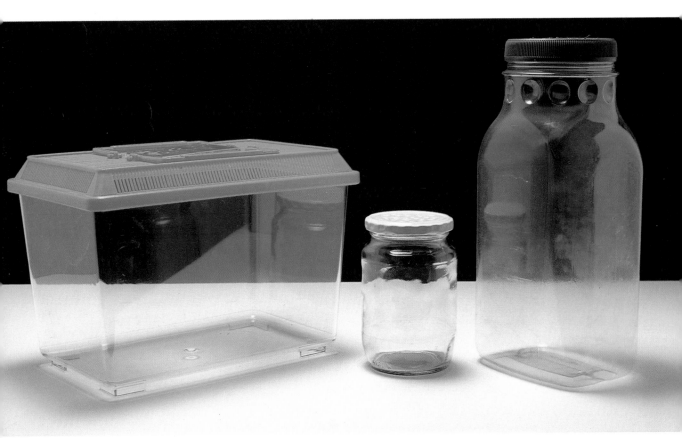

The container must not be placed in the sun
or in a draft because this will also kill the
caterpillars. A shaded windowsill in your house
is the ideal spot.

The best way to house your caterpillars is in a net cage. You can buy one to fit over a small potted plant but why not make your own?

You will need some black netting, 12 pieces of wood, nails, glue and drawing pins. The cage can be made to whatever size you want.

This type of cage is normally used for large caterpillars, because they prefer to feed on their own, away from other caterpillars and they need a lot of space.

Caterpillar food

You can feed caterpillars on either cut food or living plants. Cut food must be given fresh every day and leaves must be clean and free from chemical sprays or the caterpillars could die.

Birch

Apple

Privet

Willow

Nettle

Most gardens have suitable food growing in them and many caterpillars will eat apple, birch, willow, privet or nettle leaves. Keep the food fresh by placing it in a jar of wet sand.

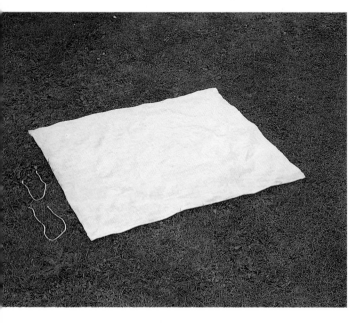

One way to feed caterpillars on growing food is to put a fabric sleeve on a tree. Sew a piece of material one meter square together to form a tube.

Place it over the end of a small branch on the tree. Tie one end with string, put the caterpillars inside and tie the other end.

Another way is to grow the food indoors like a houseplant. This should be done before you get your caterpillars so that the plant is growing strongly.

Young caterpillars

Caterpillars start life when they hatch from eggs. These are normally laid in batches on food plants that the caterpillars eat.

If there are many eggs together they will all hatch at about the same time. The first meal that a caterpillar takes is usually its own egg shell.

A caterpillar eats a large amount of food. As it grows it has to change its skin several times. When fully grown it will stop feeding and crawl away to turn into a pupa or chrysalis.

Caterpillars pupate either on the ground or on plants. They spin a silk pad to hold on to.

The caterpillar skin splits after about two days. The soft pupa hardens and the new butterfly grows inside it.

Sometimes the butterfly will emerge after just a few weeks, but others will stay in their pupae until the following year.

Releasing your caterpillars

When you release your caterpillars put them back onto their food plant or else they will starve. Do not release any foreign species or pests, such as cabbage white caterpillars.

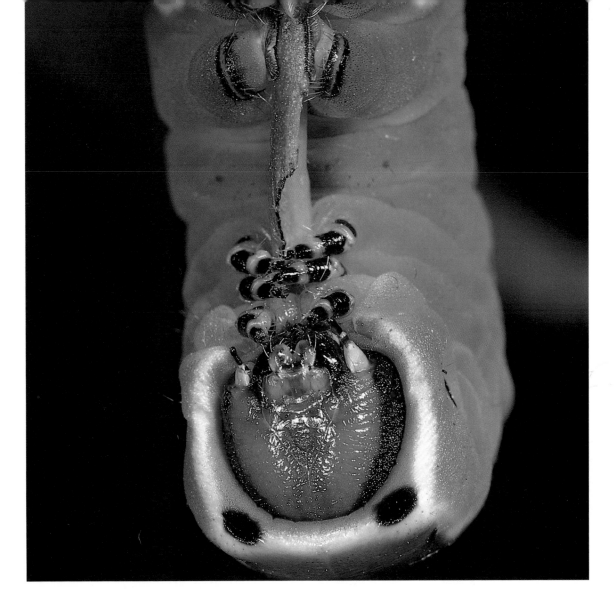

If you choose the right spot you might start your own wild breeding colony. You could check on them from time to time to see if they have turned into butterflies and laid any eggs.

Unusual facts

Some caterpillars spend the winter in hibernation. They are able to survive the coldest weather and start feeding in early spring just as the leaves appear on the trees.

A few species of caterpillar will eat their own kind, especially when they have just hatched from the egg.

The caterpillar of the Silkworm moth spins a cocoon in which to pupate. It is from this that silk cloth is made. The caterpillar makes a thread as much as a kilometer long and this is unwound to make the silk thread.

Caterpillars can not see very well as groups of tiny eyes on the sides of their head can only detect dark and light. The sense of smell is far more important.

Index

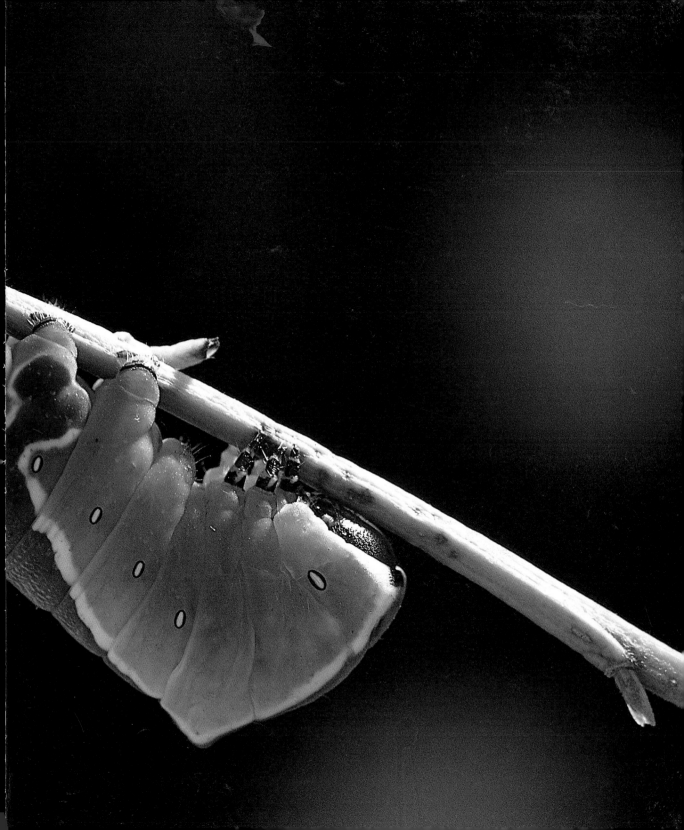